HOW BIG IS A PIG?

Clare Beaton

walk
the way of wonder...
Barefoot Books

Some cows are thin; some cows are fat.
But how big is a pig? Can you tell me that?

Some dogs are quick; some dogs are slow.
But how big is a pig? Do you think you know?

Some hens are in; some hens are out.
But how big is a pig? What's this all about?

Some frogs are jumpy; some frogs are still.
But how big is a pig? Tell me if you will!

Some cats are wild; some cats are tame.
But how big is a pig? Are they all the same?

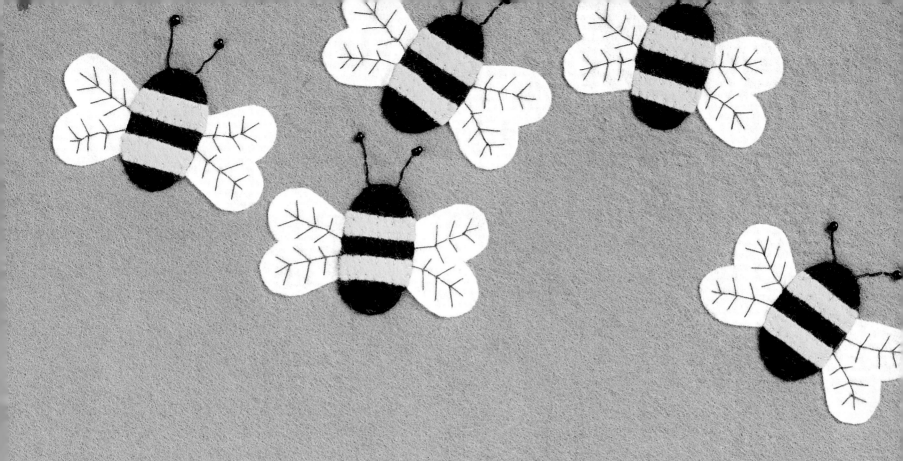

Some bees fly high; some bees fly low.
But how big is a pig? Tell me if you know!

Some geese are dirty; some geese are clean.
But how big is a pig? How many have you seen?

Some horses are young; some horses are old.
But how big is a pig? Have you been told?

Some sheep are black; some sheep are white.
But how big is a pig? Can you answer right?

Some pigs are big; some pigs are small...

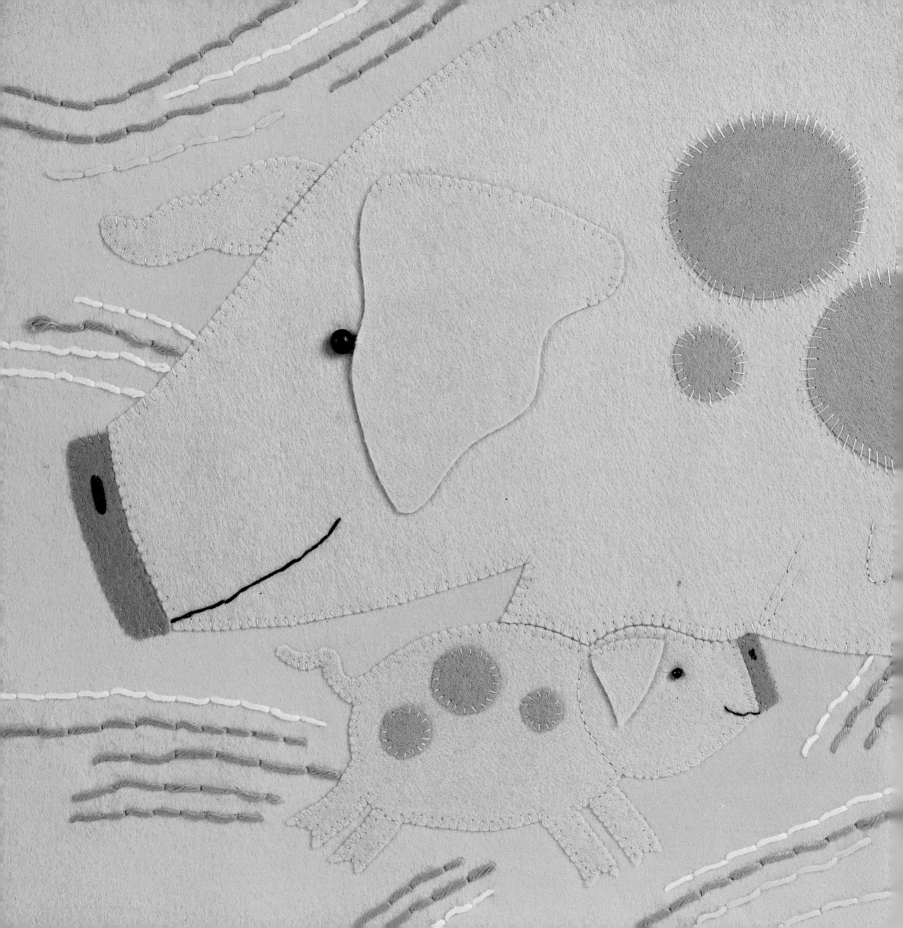

...but this pig is my mum and she's the biggest of us all!

Clare Beaton is also the illustrator of *One Moose, Twenty Mice*, *Zoë and her Zebra* and *Mother Goose Remembers*, all published by Barefoot Books.

Praise for *One Moose, Twenty Mice*:

'Clare Beaton's dazzlingly colourful felt work provides a splendid pictorial counting base in her number book, and the imaginative user will also be able to play counting games with the decorative details...Outstanding' — *Carousel*

'The illustrations are comfortably tactile and they offer some clever effects...Young viewers will find the fuzzy menagerie endearing, and they'll giggle through the rollicking kitty hunt' — *Bulletin of the Center for Children's Books*

'The simple satisfaction of playing the game and the pleasure of the illustrations guarantee that this counting book will hold children's interest longer than most. A good participation book for nursery school story hour' — *Booklist*

For my younger son, Tom – C. B.

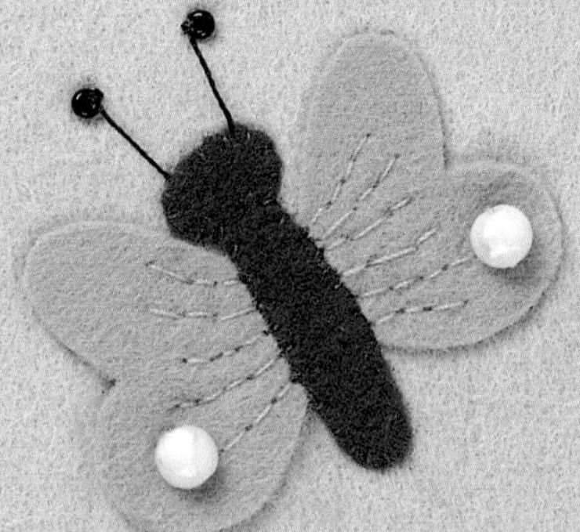

Barefoot Books
PO Box 95
Kingswood
Bristol
BS30 5BH

Text copyright © 2000 by Stella Blackstone
Illustrations copyright © 2000 by Clare Beaton
The moral right of Stella Blackstone to be identified as the author and Clare Beaton
to be identified as the illustrator of this work has been asserted

This book was typeset in Plantin Schoolbook Bold 20 on 28 point
The illustrations were prepared in felt with braid, beads and sequins

Graphic design by Judy Linard, London
Colour transparencies by Jonathan Fisher Photography, Bath
Colour separation by Grafiscan, Verona
Printed and bound in Singapore by Tien Wah Press Pte Ltd

This book has been printed on 100% acid-free paper

Hardback ISBN 1 84148 076 2
Paperback ISBN 1 84148 078 9

British Cataloguing-in-Publication Data: a catalogue record for this book is available from the British Library

1 3 5 7 9 8 6 4 2

walk
the way of wonder...
Barefoot Books

The barefoot child symbolizes the human being who is in harmony with the natural world and moves freely across boundaries of many kinds. Barefoot Books explores this image with a range of high-quality picture books for children of all ages. We work with artists, writers, and storytellers from many cultures, focusing on themes that encourage independence of spirit, promote understanding and acceptance of different traditions, and foster a life-long love of learning.
www.barefoot-books.com